HOW TO READ

THE GREEK NEW TESTAMENT

Prepared primarily for those who are unacquainted with the Greek language, but who desire to be able to locate every word in the Greek New Testament, trace it to its root, define it, and parse the sentence in which it occurs.

By GUY N. WOODS

Other books by Guy N. Woods include commentaries on John, James, 1 and 2 Peter, 1, 2, and 3 John and Jude.

GOSPEL ADVOCATE CO.

P. O. Box 150

Nashville, Tennessee 37202

HOW TO READ THE GREEK NEW TESTAMENT

Copyright, 1970

By GUY N. WOODS

Reprinted November 1984

INTRODUCTION

This series of lessons on How To Read The Greek New Testament has been primarily prepared for those who are unacquainted with the Greek language, but who wish to read and to study the New Testament in its original form.

This work does not affect to be a Grammar of New Testament Greek, a treatment of Greek syntax, or a book of definitions. It establishes a verbal connection between the English language and the Greek New Testament, so that one, without previous training in Greek is able to locate every word in the Greek New Testament, trace the word to its root, define the word, and parse the sentence in which the word appears!

The work therefore, in this respect, is unique. Nothing like it exists. It is truly a shortcut to the study of New Testament Greek. *An average student, possessing only an elementary knowledge of English, by a few days of careful study of the system herein taught, may make his own translation from the language in which the New Testament was written into his own tongue!* Aside from the study of the New Testament itself, no exercise enriches the mind, stirs the heart, and increases the efficiency of the teacher or preacher of God's word so much as does diligent and daily search in the language in which the Holy Spirit gave the message of life and salvation to the world. Not all of us have the time nor the inclination to become *scholars*, but we can all be *scholarly* — studious — and we owe it to ourselves, to those whom we would influence, and to God to equip ourselves for the greatest capability possible.

Nearly thirty years ago, in response to many requests, this writer published a small book on "How To Use The Greek New Testament," but the edition was soon exhausted and has long been out of print and unobtainable. We are happy to bring out an enlarged, revised and improved edition of the work which we earnestly hope will aid many in our day to mine the rich ores of the New Testament as did the earlier work.

It is believed that those who are trained in Greek will find this course stimulating and inspirational; and that those not interested in studying the Greek text, as such, will find the 99 passages expounded in this series of studies interesting and edifying.

October 1, 1978

P. O. Box 150   GUY N. WOODS
Nashville, Tenn. 37202

CONTENTS

PART ONE

PART TWO

PART THREE

PART ONE
THE SYSTEM INTRODUCED

LESSON 1

WHY WE SHOULD STUDY THE GREEK NEW TESTAMENT

The debt we owe to the scholarship of the world for having made available to us such excellent translations of the sacred writings is indeed a weighty one. The race has been blessed by the labors and skill of many great men in this worthy field of endeavor, and for their efforts we should be, and are, profoundly grateful.

But, notwithstanding the excellence of their productions, it remains that they have given us nothing more than *translations*—translations encumbered with the imperfections which inevitably attach themselves to every effort to transfer thought from one language to another. All scholars are aware of the fact that the fullness, the power, and the richness of the original can never be adequately conveyed in translation, and there perishes in the effort that fleeting, indescribable something available only to those who can read in the original tongue.

The words of one language are never precisely

9

the same in meaning as those of another, and it is for this reason impossible for an English translation of the New Testament exactly to reproduce the Greek text. Their forms and idioms differ, the corresponding words of each language are never exactly the same, and a translation from one to the other can only approximate the meaning of the original statement.

The effort to transfer the meaning of the text from one language to another by translation is comparable to playing music on a violin which was originally written for the piano. While in such an attempt it is possible to reproduce the melody, yet the subtle undertones intended by the composer are lost, and other effects are injected in the rendition not anticipated by him.

As the loveliest picture of human art cannot compare with the majesty and inexpressible sublimity of nature, so no translation, however excellent, can give the finer shades of thought, the ease of expression, and the deeper beauties of meaning discoverable in the sacred text.

The ability to read the New Testament in the language in which it was originally written, and to discover for oneself the precious gems embedded in its rich mines of truth, is truly an acquisition priceless in value to the devout and conscientious Bible student and expositor. The effort, even in its primary stages, is valuable; and the amazed and delighted student from the beginning becomes thrillingly conscious of a new and mighty power in his hands in teaching and preaching the Divine Oracles. He will at once begin to feel as Erasmus expressed it in the Preface of his Greek Testament over four hundred years ago: "These holy pages will summon up the living image of His mind. They will give you Christ himself, talking, healing, dying, rising, the whole Christ in a word; they will give Him to you in an intimacy so close that He would be less visible to you if He stood before your eyes."

The perpetual "remainders of precious truth left untranslated," which every student of the Greek New Testament knows to abound in its sacred pages are within reach of only those who are able to make their way in the original language. To mine these rich ores of truth, and make them shine and sparkle for one's hearers is surely the most fascinating and delightful of all studies. A preacher or Bible school teacher

11

who is able to do this will always exhibit a freshness and charm that will delight and thrill his hearers, and he may be sure that they will return again and again to listen as he brings out of this inexhaustible Storehouse of Truth, its rare and precious treasures.

One who must rely on the translations can never speak with authority on matters pertaining to the text. He must always depend on what others have said that the text means. He can never hope to escape the feeling of inadequacy and inferiority which inevitably descends upon him, when any question arises touching the original writings. It is impossible for him to answer satisfactorily and with firsthand information the many questions which arise as a result of comparing the King James and American Standard Versions. But having acquired such information, he is like a traveler who, after a long and wearisome journey, is at last able to see with his own eyes, and walk with his own feet in the Blessed Land where the Word was made flesh and tabernacled among men!

Surely the faithful and conscientious Bible expositor will not be satisfied with less than the best he has to offer in his efforts to expound the Word; and it is now so easy to acquire a working knowledge of the Greek Testament that a failure to do so must be regarded as evidence of lassitude and indifference in the most vital matter challenging the attention of men.

Erasmus, the mighty Greek scholar of the Reformation, wrote to a friend while working his way through the University of Paris: "I have given up my whole soul to Greek learning, and as soon as I can get any money, I shall buy Greek books *and then clothes.*" Is it to be wondered at that this man became the greatest Greek scholar of the Reformation?

The world famous Scottish theologian, John Brown of Haddington, was brought up an orphan, and worked as a shepherd lad on the hills of Scotland. He was ambitious to master the Greek language, but was too poor to buy either a grammar or lexicon. He borrowed a Greek Testament, and laboriously learned the alphabet from the proper names in the genealogies of the Lord recorded in Matthew and Luke. Anxious to have a Greek Testament of his own, and having over long months saved his pitiful wages until he had enough to buy a cheap copy, he left his flock with

13

a friend one night, and walked twenty-four miles to the nearest town where such a book could be purchased, arriving just as the store opened for the day. By afternoon, he was back with his sheep, avidly poring over his newly obtained treasure. He was sixteen years old at this time, and lived to be regarded as one of the world's greatest Greek scholars.

Phillips Brooks was one of the most eminent men of his day, and his scholarship in the field of New Testament exegesis was thorough and extensive. It is said of him that he dealt with the Greek of the New Testament in such fashion that "it rejoiced like Enoch in being translated!"

Wesley was unquestionably right when he said, "A guide to souls ought to know the literal meaning of every word, verse, and chapter in Scripture; without which there can be no firm foundation on which the spiritual meaning can be built . . . Can he do this, in the most effectual manner, without a knowledge of the original tongues? Without this will he not frequently be at a stand, even as to texts which regard practice only? But he will be under still greater difficulties, with respect to controverted scriptures. He will be ill able to rescue these out of the hands of any man of learning that would pervert them: for whenever an appeal is made to the original, his mouth is stopped at once."

Finally, it is worthy of note that the critical commentaries embody the results of many centuries of minute, laborious, and detailed study, little of which the student can grasp who does not have a working knowledge of the Greek language. Such a one is thus barred from using matter of an indispensable and invaluable nature from this source, and must depend on others to make available to him the fruits of such study and learning. As a matter of fact, one able to work in the Greek Testament may, in large measure, dispense with much of the material on which he has hitherto had to depend. Often a short and easy method is found to the meaning of the text, where before this result could have been obtained only after a lengthy and detailed examination of the authorities. What the commentator must explain in many words, and with much expansion of the original thought, the Greek often vividly and graphically points to in few words. In truth it can be said that the clearest, simplest, most vivid, and most inspiring commentary on the New Testament in English is, to one who can use it, the New Testament in Greek! An elderly women, a lifelong student of the Word, borrowed some com-

15

mentaries from her preacher. When she returned them, she said, "These are good books. I find that the Bible throws much light on them." The Greek New Testament throws light on the Word one cannot get from a translation. Evidence of this will follow.

EXERCISE 1

1. Obtain a notebook in which to write down the impressions and suggestions from these lessons. Outline the material under each division, and designate the lesson in which such appears. Leave room for additional notes which you will wish to add in later studies. Your notes will thus become an invaluable aid to you later.

2. State, in one hundred words or less, why it is not always possible for the translations to express the full significance of the original test.

3. Write out, in your own words, what is said in the illustrations taken from music and art.

4. Why is the ability to read the Greek New Testament such a great blessing? What did

16

Erasmus, the great Reformation scholar, say about this?

5. Why is one who knows no Greek at a disadvantage? Read carefully the comments about Erasmus, John Brown, Phillips Brooks, John Wesley.

6. What vast store of information available to Greek students cannot be used by those who know no Greek?

7. What is the clearest, simplest, most vivid and most inspiring commentary on the New Testament?

8. Read Lesson 1, until you are thoroughly familiar with its contents, and transfer to your note book all essential points.

LESSON 2

EXAMPLES OF GREEK EXEGESIS

In 1 Peter 2:21, the apostle declares that Christ left us an "example," that we should walk in his steps. Here, the word "example" is from the Greek ὑπογραμμόν, accusative singular of ὑπογραμμός, from the preposition ὑπο-, under;

17

and γράμμα, to write: thus, literally, to *write under*. Its meaning is "a copy to write after," and metaphorically, "an example for imitation, pattern" (Bagster) ; and "a writing copy . . . hence, an example." (Thayer.) The word is thus a figure of speech, suggested by the copy-book method of teaching penmanship. How vividly does this point up the meaning of the inspired apostle! We see in his word a copy-book, a specimen of beautiful writing at the top of the page, a white, unblemished sheet of paper, the student's effort to transcribe the copy, the awkward attempts in the beginning, the persistent determination, the constant and unremitting practice; and then, eventually—success!

The application is obvious and fitting. Christ is our copy-head—the beautiful writing at the top of the page. The life we live represents our effort to copy Him, and the manner of it, the degree of success we have attained in the attempt. If we are appalled, yea, dismayed by the vast difference which obtains between our own feeble, imperfect attempts to imitate Him, and the perfect example that He is, let us remember that the slow, laborious and awkward efforts of the beginning penman are not by him regarded as the ultimate in achievement. The sensible student does not, on viewing his first, clumsy and imperfect attempts, fling aside his pen in despair, and say, "I never can learn to write." He recognizes that with practice comes proficiency, and that eventually he will attain to a degree of success impossible to him in the beginning.

This rich background, and much more, is immediately apparent to the Greek student in the word translated *example* in this text. How very few of these interesting implications are available to the English student alone.

We may be sure that every word in the Greek Testament is equally brimming with suggestive and illustrative material, ready to contribute its share in the Divine Revelation to those who possess the ingenuity to find it, and the perseverance essential to the effort. Let us examine another instance from the same context in 1 Peter 2. To encourage the saints in the fiery trials of persecution through which they were passing, Peter penned these words, "For so it is the will of God, that with well-doing ye may put to silence the ignorance of foolish men. . . ." (1 Peter 2:15.)

The verb of the second clause, rendered "put to silence" in the translation, is from the Greek φιμοῦν, present infinitive active, of φιμόω, liter-

19

ally, *to muzzle!* Metaphorically, and by implication, it means to silence. (Bagster.) Instances of its literal meaning, and where it is thus literally rendered are in 1 Cor. 9:9 and 1 Tim. 5:18. The Christian is admonished by the apostle to muzzle foolish men who wickedly accuse them; and the muzzle to be used is the Christian's own good deeds! In this way, all evil men who bark at them, or who would bite them, find themselves restrained by the good works of the faithful. As a muzzle renders a vicious and ill-tempered dog harmless, so the godly behavior of Christians effectively muzzles their most malevolent foes! In one word we are thus enabled to see the picture of wicked men effectively restrained in their efforts to harm the Lord's people by being muzzled, like vicious and growling curs, by the faithfulness and fidelity characteristic of Christians.

How much more vivid is the term Peter uses than the very commonplace translation by which it is rendered in the English versions! When Jesus said, "Till heaven and earth pass one jot or one tittle shall in no wise pass from the law, till all be fulfilled" (Matt. 5:17), did he not mean that even the smallest portions, the apparently most insignificant parts of the divine revelation are essential and necessary to complete his will to man?

In a thrilling passage in the Roman Letter, Paul tells us that "the earnest expectation of the creature waiteth for the manifestation of the sons of God." (Rom. 8:19.) The word "expectation" is translated from the long, compound word, ἀποκαραδοκία. It is composed of three roots, ἀπό, *from, from afar;* κάρα, *the head;* and δοκεύω, *to wait for.* Thus the word suggests the idea of one who waits with his head raised, and his eyes steadfastly fixed on the point in the distance from which the expected object will appear. We may see it in the man who stands on the station platform, anxiously bending forward to catch the first glimpse of the oncoming engine as it appears around the bend. How little of this appears in our English word *expectation.*

The verb in this sentence, ἀπεκδέχεται, translated "waiteth for," is equally interesting and significant. It is made up of the verb δέχομαι, *to receive,* and the two prepositions, ἐκ, *out of,* and ἀπό, *from, from afar.* It thus suggests the idea of receiving something from the hands of another who extends it from a distance. By joining the thoughts embedded in the noun and the verb of the sentence whose meanings we have just considered, we catch the picture of a groaning, sin-afflicted creation, standing, as it were, on tip-toe, and looking

21

eagerly along the vista of the years, for the first faint gleams which presage the day of deliverance. How much more vivid and correct is this than the passive idea inherent in the rendering "expectation," which represents creation as having insipidly folded its hands and sat down to "wait for," the coming manifestation. The waiting suggested in the verb is not passive lassitude and idle indifference. Thayer says that it means to "assiduously and patiently wait for." The word occurs in Phil. 3:20, where it is translated "look for," indicating the intense feeling characteristic of those who watch for the coming of the Lord from glory.

Gal. 1:6, 7, as it appears in the King James or "Authorized" version, is meaningless and contradictory. There, Paul is made to refer to *another* gospel which he immediately declares is not *an other* gospel! How could the doctrine of the Judaizing teachers, to whom he refers in this passage, be another gospel when it is not another? This poses a problem which the English reader, relying solely on the common version, could never solve. The passage is shrouded in impenetrable mystery as it stands in the translation above alluded to.

A mere glance at the Greek text solves the problem. The word "another," is the translation of *two different* Greek words in verses 6 and 7. The "another" gospel of the false teachers was an ἕτερος gospel (a gospel of a different kind) and not an ἄλλος gospel (a gospel of the same kind). The gospel the Judaizers preached was therefore a gospel of an entirely different character from that which the apostles preached, and hence without its saving power. (Rom. 1:16.) Because the English language is not as discriminating as the Greek, it is not always possible to exhibit such sharp distinctions in translation without resorting to a whole sentence or paragraph to reveal the meaning of one word or phrase; and since such is not permissible in a translation, such distinctions are often lost to the English reader.

In Romans 3:2, 3, one Greek root occurs four times; yet, the King James Translators rendered it by four different words, and the English reader could never know that there was any lexical connection. The passage reads: "Unto them were committed (ἐπιστεύθησαν, third person plural, of the aorist indicative passive of πιστεύω, from πίστις, faith) the oracles of God. For what if some did not believe (derived from πίστις, faith) shall their unbelief (from πίστις, faith) make the faith (πίστις) of God without effect?" From the King

23

James rendering how could one have known that *committed, believe, unbelief,* and *faith* in this passage were all derived from the same source? This reveals most pointedly that which the reader must by now surely be impressed with, that no translation, however excellent, can suggest all the richness of detail and vividness of expression characteristic of the original writings.

For example, in a familiar passage in Hebrews, we read, "And others were tortured not accepting deliverance." (Heb. 11:35.) Of the mode and nature of the torture, the translation gives no inkling; and yet, the matter is clear in the Greek text. The verb is ἐτυμπανίσθησαν, from τύμπανον, "a wheel shaped instrument of torture, over which criminals were stretched as though they were skins, and then horribly beaten with clubs or thongs." (Thayer.) Despite the slow and terrible torture to which they were subjected they never wavered; they never accepted the deliverance their tormentors offered them at various stages of the torture; they endured being sure that they would obtain a better resurrection. The real triumph of their faith and the genuine heroism they manifested in the face of their persecutors thus becomes especially apparent in the Greek text.

John 11:35 is the shortest verse in the Bible, "Jesus wept." We have, perhaps from childhood, visualized the Savior sobbing, weeping audibly with the grief-stricken sisters of Lazarus. We were wrong. The word "wept" is translated from the verb ἐδάκρυσεν, 3 pers. sing. aorist indicative active, of δακρύω, to shed tears, to weep silently. (Thayer.) However, in Luke 19:41, where Jesus "wept over" the city of Jerusalem, the word is ἔκλαυσεν, from κλαίω, "to weep audibly, to cry as a child." In Bethany Jesus shed tears silently; over Jerusalem he sobbed in bitter lamentation over the fallen and rebellious city. Limitations of space forbid further illustration of the value of Greek study; but when the reader has mastered Parts Two and Three of this work, he will then be able to continue his study in what is surely the most thrilling and valuable pursuit possible to man.

EXERCISE 2

1. Lesson 2 contains numerous examples of the value of Greek exegesis. Here, we illustrate what *may* be done; later, the student will be doing this, himself!

2. Write out I Pet. 2:21, in your notebook. Copy exactly the Greek word, translated "example." Note that the word literally designates, "A copy to write after," "An example for imitation, pattern," ... "A writing copy...hence, an example." Note the figure on which the statement is based. Write out what we see in this, and the application. Be thorough.

3. Deal similarly with I Pet. 2:15. Make the application. Observe how a knowledge of the Greek word translated "muzzle," here enriches, and vivifies the text for us. Give significance of Matt. 5:17.

4. Explain Rom. 8:19, in the light of the Greek text. What vivid impression do we receive from the word translated "expectation." Give the three roots, and the idea suggested. Describe the verb translated "waiteth for," and make the application.

5. Without a knowledge of the Greek text, is it possible to explain how "another gospel" is not "another?" (Gal. 1:6,7.) What is the simple explanation found in the Greek text?

6. What remarkable situation exists in Rom. 3:2,3? Explain Heb. 11:35. What light does the Greek text shed on John 11:35? Luke 19:41?

PART TWO

THE SYSTEM EXPLAINED

LESSON 3

We shall endeavor, in Parts Two and Three of this work, to exhibit to the reader a system whereby one who has some knowledge of English, but who does not know one Greek letter from another, may in a few hours, by perseverance and concentrated study, learn how to locate every word in the Greek Testament, trace it to its root, define it, parse the sentence in which it occurs, and note its grammatical relationship.

This does not mean that one can become a polished Greek scholar overnight, or that it is possible in a few hours to master the Greek language. Such can be done only by the unremitting toil and the ceaseless effort of a lifetime.

It does mean that with reasonable effort and some perseverance, an average student who knows no Greek will be able to make his way in the text of the Greek New Testament by following the suggestions herein set forth. It is to be hoped that many who, in this manner, obtain some morsels of the delectable delights of that wonderful Feast, will be prompted to go on to the mastery of the language in which the Words of Life were vouch-safed to the world.

The student will need *two* books to pursue the studies outlined in this book. These are (1) an interlinear New Testament, a book containing the Greek text, and a literal English translation under each Greek word; and (2) The Analytical Greek Lexicon, a wonderful volume absolutely indispensable to the Greek student, whether he be a beginner or a mature student, containing every inflected form of every word in the Greek New Testament, traced to its root and defined. Most preachers have, or can easily obtain, Berry's Interlinear, and this writer will be glad to inform inquirers where both of these volumes may be reasonably purchased.

The steps which follow are exceedingly simple, but they are absolutely necessary, and they must be thoroughly mastered. After the careful study of this book, the average student should, with the helps suggested, be able to make his way satisfactorily in the text of the Greek Testament. The ability to make one's own translation of the passages he chooses to study is the goal, and for its attainment no effort is too great.

30

The first step in the process is to learn the letters of the Greek alphabet. It is suggested that the small, or common, letters be learned first, the capitals being learned after the student has made his way through the book. Most Greek words are spelled out with small letters, and the Lexicons list them in this manner; hence the learning of the capitals may be deferred until the system is mastered.

There are twenty-four letters in the Greek alphabet. There is much diversity of opinion regarding the proper sound of some of these letters, and as it is impossible now to know how the ancient Greeks pronounced them, it is best to consider each letter as corresponding in sound to the equivalent letter in the English alphabet. There are seven diphthongs: $\alpha\iota$ *ai* as in aisle; $\alpha\upsilon$ *au* as in naught; $\epsilon\iota$ *ei* as in height; $\omicron\iota$ *oi* as in oil; $\omicron\upsilon$ *ou* as in out; $\epsilon\upsilon$ and $\eta\upsilon$ *eu* as in neuter; and $\upsilon\iota$ as *wi* in wine. ('Note: some Greek grammars give the pronunciation of $\epsilon\iota$ as long $\bar{a}$, but the older grammars without exception prefer the pronunciation given above.)

It is suggested that the student copy the letters of the alphabet until he can write them with ease and recognize them readily. For practice he should try his hand at pronouncing words in the Greek Testament. The accent is immaterial at this stage of the process.

THE GREEK ALPHABET

CAPITALS	SMALL LETTERS		NAME	ENGLISH EQUIVALENT
A	α		Alpha	a as in father
B	β		Beta	b as in bat
Γ	γ		Gamma	g as in get
Δ	δ		Delta	d as in done
E	ε	(short)	Epsilon	e as in met
Z	ζ		Zeta	z as in zebra
H	η	(long)	Eta	e as in they
Θ	θ		Theta	th as in thing
I	ι		Iota	i as in machine
K	κ		Kappa	k as in king
Λ	λ		Lambda	l as in let
M	μ		Mu	m as in must
N	ν		Nu	n as in no
Ξ	ξ		Xi	x as in example
O	ο	(short)	Omicron	o as in obey
Π	π		Pi	p as in pet
P	ρ		Rho	r as in ring

Σ	σ ς**		Sigma	s as in sing
T	τ		Tau	t as in time
Υ	υ		Upsilon	*
Φ	φ		Phi	ph as in phase
X	χ		Chi	ch as in chasm
Ψ	ψ		Psi	ps as in lips
Ω	ω	(long)	Omega	o as in tone

The vowels of the Greek alphabet are ε, η, ο, ω, α, ι, υ.

Each Greek word beginning with a vowel has a mark resembling a comma over it. If the comma is turned the usual way, the vowel is unaspirated. If the comma is reversed, the vowel is said to be aspirated, and given the "h" sound of the English language. For example, ἥλιος (sun) is pronounced as if spelled *helios,* while ἐπι (upon) is pronounced simply "epi."

When a word begins with a diphthong, the comma always stands over the second vowel. υἱος (son) is pronounced *why-os.*

Whenever the letter *gamma* (γ) appears before another γ, it is always pronounced like "n." ἀγγελος (angel) is pronounced *angelos,* not *aggelos.*

---

* The υ is guttural, somewhat like the e in key.
** σ in the middle of the word, but ς at the close.

33

Accents are used to indicate the syllable upon which stress is to be laid in pronunciation.

EXERCISE 3

1. What is the design of this series of lessons, and what may the student, by reasonable effort and some perseverance, expect to accomplish?

2. In order to *continue* the study of the Greek Testament when this course is finished, the student will need an *interlinear New Testament,* which has in it the Greek text, a literal word-for-word translation, and the King James' Version; and The Analytical Greek Lexicon. These two volumes ought to be in the library of *every* student of the scriptures, and it would be well to obtain them as soon as possible.

3. Learn the letters of the Greek alphabet, and be able to give their Greek names, ie., alpha, beta, gamma, etc. From the table given, learn the correct pronunciation of the letters and the vowels. Copy them until you are able to do so easily and quickly. Learn to look for the mark resembling a comma, note its position, and pronounce the word accordingly. Note what it is said

about the letter gamma. Observe accents, and pronounce accordingly.

Turn to lesson 7, and (a) spell the Greek words from Matt. 7:7; (b) note carefully the vowels and the consonants, and give them their proper sounds; (c) observe accent and pronounce the words correctly. In transliterating Greek words (spelling them out in English), don't bother to spell them by calling their Greek names; designate them by their English equivalents, that is, in spelling the Greek word ἐκκλησία (ekklesia) we are not to say epsilon, kappa, kappa, lambda, sigma, iota, alpha; we would simply spell it out as *ekklesia*, thus given the English equivalents of the Green letters.

The student should devote several days to Lesson 3, and thoroughly learn it. The alphabet is basic to the study of Greek; one, who would become skilled in mathematics, must learn how to add, subtract, and multiply!

Observe that some of the letters have long and short forms; note that sigma has a different form when used at the close of a word.

35

LESSON 4

Greek is an *inflected* language. *Inflection* is the change that is made in words, by the addition of letters, to indicate the variations of case, mood, tense, number, etc. The *stem* is that part of the word which remains virtually the same through all the varieties of inflection. Nouns, Adjectives, and Pronouns are *declined,* and Verbs are *conjugated* by prefixes or terminations added to the stem. The *stem* contains the main idea of the word, and is traceable to the *root,* from which all words of the same family are derived.

To illustrate the manner in which words indicate their properties of case, tense, number, etc., through inflection, we take the word λύω, *I loose,* first person singular, of the present indicative active. The stem is λύ-, and the sign of the first person singular of the present indicative active is -ω.

PRESENT INDICATIVE ACTIVE OF λύω

SINGULAR

1. λύω, I loose
2. λύεις, you loose
3. λύει, he looses

PLURAL

1. λύομεν, we loose
2. λύετε, you loose
3. λύουσι, they loose

FUTURE INDICATIVE ACTIVE OF λύω

1. λύσω, I shall loose
2. λύσις, you shall loose
3. λύσει, he shall loose

1. λύσομεν, we shall loose
2. λύσετε, you shall loose
3. λύσουσι, they shall loose

IMPERFECT INDICATIVE ACTIVE OF λύω

1. ἔλυον, I was loosing
2. ἔλυες, you were loosing
3. ἔλυε, he was loosing

1. ἐλύομεν, we were loosing
2. ἐλύετε, you were loosing
3. ἔλυον, they were loosing

Thus, by the addition of letters to the stem, words are modified to indicate case, tense, mood, number, etc. The Analytical Greek Lexicon lists in alphabetical order every inflection occurring in the New Testament, and it is therefore unnecessary to give all the tables here. These examples are given to acquaint the student with the structure of the Greek word.

As an illustration of the inflection characteristic of nouns, note carefully the declension of ἐκκλησία, *the church.*

1. ἐκκλησία, nominative singular, the church.
2. ἐκκλησίαι, nominative plural, the churches.
3. ἐκκλησίᾳ, dative singular, in, or with, the church.
4. ἐκκλησίαις, dative plural, in, or with, the churches.
5. ἐκκλησίας, genitive singular, of the church.
6. ἐκκλησιῶν, genitive plural, of the churches.
7. ἐκκλησίαν, accusative singular, to the church.
8. ἐκκλησίας, accusative plural, to the churches.

THE CASES

There are five cases:

1. The Nominative, the case of the subject.
2. The Genitive, the possessive or "whence" case.
3. The Dative, the case of sphere, or location, the "where" case.
4. The Accusative, or case of the object.
5. The Vocative, the case of direct address.*

As in English, the verb agrees with the subject

---

*Some recent grammars add to the genitive, the ablative; and to the dative, the instrumental case. For the beginner it is preferable to follow the older arrangement given above.

in number and person; the Greek article must be in the same gender, number and case, as the noun to which it belongs; and the genitive, dative and accusative are often governed by prepositions conforming to the nature of the case to which they are attached, i.e., the genitive signifying origin, *from;* the dative, association, *in* or *with;* and the accusative, approach, *towards, to, into.*

The position of emphasis in a sentence is at the beginning or end. All nouns in Greek are either masculine, feminine, or neuter gender. The Greek of the New Testament has two numbers: singular and plural.

THE VERB

There are *five* Moods in Greek:

1. The Indicative, which says or asks: *He seeks. Does he seek?*

2. The Imperative, which commands: *Seek ye.*

3. The Subjunctive, conditional, sometimes a question: *If he seek?*

4. The Optative, properly a division of the Subjunctive, which expresses a wish: *May he seek.*

5. The Infinitive, which expresses the action or

state indicated by the verb, as itself an object of thought: *To love is divine.* The infinitive is sometimes styled a verbal noun.

There are *three* Voices in Greek:

1. Active: *To love.*
2. Passive: *To be loved.*
3. Middle: *To love oneself.*

The active and passive voices are identical with those in English. The middle voice indicates that the subject is in some way acting upon itself.

There are *three* Persons:

SINGULAR	PLURAL
1. First Person: *I* seek.	1. First Person: *We* seek.
2. Second Person: *You* seek.	2. Second Person: *You* seek.
3. Third Person: *He* seeks.	3. Third Person: *They* seek.

In most lexicons and vocabularies, the first person singular, of the present indicative active, is given. This is true of Thayer, Robinson, Green, Parkhurst, etc. We shall later see how, by following the system herein taught, one may take any inflected form, regardless of how much modification it may have undergone in inflection, and trace it to its root.

EXERCISE 4

1. Note the Greek is an inflected language. Learn thoroughly what inflection is; the stem; the root; and observe, from the table given, how that by the addition of letters to the stem, words are modified to indicate case, tense, mood, number, etc. The student will not need to master this table; it is given for illustration only. The Analytical Lexicon will provide, in alphebetical order, every word, and every inflection of every word occurring in the Greek New Testament! Examine the inflection of the word *ecclesia,* translated "church."

2. Learn thoroughly the significance of the cases; the position of emphasis and the three genders used in the Greek New Testament.

3. Master the moods, and the three voices. Note that the middle voice (which does not occur in English), indicates that the subject is in some way acting upon itself. Take note that the three persons are identical with English usage.

41

4. Observe that in most lexicons (Greek dictionaries), the first person singular of the present indicative active, is the form given. For this reason, and because Greek words undergo great changes in form in inflection, it is not possible to go directly from the Greek Testament to the lexicon in ascertaining the meaning of a Greek word, if one knows no Greek; but the student who pursues this course will be able easily to do so in a few days, having learned how to trace words, however great their modification in inflection, to their root and determine their meaning.

LESSON 5

THE GREEK TENSES

One of the first, and indeed, one of the most important things to learn in the study of Greek is the significance of the tenses. The word *tense,* from the French "temps," is misleading if we are to take it in its usual signification, for the word signifies time, and originally the Greek tense had no reference to time. This characteristic, so prominent in the English verb, is only incidental in the Greek.

The tense in Greek has to do with the state of

the action, according as it is conceived of as an indefinite event, as action in progress, or as completed action with existing results.

In English, the time element is prominent, and we think of an event as either past, present, or future. It must be remembered that in Greek the tense indicates the kind of action that is characteristic of the verb, and the time element is only incidental thereto. This is a fundamental difference between the Greek and English verb, and one that must be kept constantly in mind in translating the Greek verb into English.

There are seven tenses in the Indicative Mood: The Present and Imperfect, which denote action continued or repeated; the Aorist and Future indicate indefinite action, and the Perfect, Pluperfect, and Future Perfect denote action completed.

The *Present Tense* indicates action in progress at the present time. It thus distinguishes itself from the *Aorist*, a single act indefinitely conceived of without regard to time.

1. Present tense: λύω, *I am loosing,* a continuous act in progress at the present time.
2. Aorist tense: ἔλυσα, *I loosed,* a single act without regard to time.
3. Imperfect tense: ἔλυον, *I was loosing,* an act

43

in progress in past time and continuing.

4. Future tense: λύσω, *I shall loose,* action yet future.

The pluperfect and the future perfect tenses are similar in meaning to those in English, bearing in mind the essential difference in the nature of the tenses in the languages emphasized above.

The difference between the present and the aorist may be seen in the following manner:

The *present* tense: (————) , an act continuing.
The *aorist* tense: (.) , a single act.

The vividness of detail possible in Greek appears in the following passage: "Jesus answered and said unto her, Whosoever drinketh (πίνων, present participle of πίνω, to drink, thus literally, to keep on drinking) of this water shall thirst again, but whoso drinketh (πίῃ, aorist subjunctive, to take a single drink) of the water that I shall give him shall never thirst. . . ." (John 4:13, 14.) Expanded to indicate the force of these tenses, the translation runs: "Whosoever *keeps on drinking* of this water shall thirst again; but whoso takes *a single drink* of the water that I shall give him shall never thirst. . . ." It was necessary for those who drank from the water of the well in Samaria to

44

return again and again; it could quench the thirst for short periods only. But, those who drank from the Well of Life eternal found the waters thereof ever satisfying! Constant drinking from worldly wells can never permanently quench the thirst, but one drink from the Well of which Jesus spoke satisfies forever. In this connection it is interesting to note that the Greek text (but not the English) distinguishes between the *well* of Samaria and the *Well* of water springing up into everlasting life. The first is φρέαρ, a cistern into which water seeps and becomes stagnant; the second is πηγὴ, a spring from which fresh and living waters flow. The water of salvation never grows stale. The waters of the world all eventually become brackish and unsatisfying.

In Mark 2:9, Jesus said to the man sick of palsy, "Arise, and take up thy bed and walk." *Arise* and *take up thy bed* are, in the Greek, aorist imperatives. *Walk*, however, is present imperative. Thus, Jesus bade the man to get up, pick up his bed in a single act, and start walking and keep on walking!

An interesting and significant difference between the present and the aorist tenses occurs in the clash between Paul and Barnabas over John

45

Mark. (Acts 15:37). John Mark had turned back on a former tour, and now that another journey was contemplated, Barnabas proposed that they take Mark along with them again. In making the proposal, Barnabas used the aorist infinitive, συνπαραλαβεῖν. It is as if he said, "Let's take him along one more time." Paul answered with the present infinitive, μή συνπαραλαμβάνειν. "What! *Keep on* taking him along?" the apostle implied in his reply. Paul had not forgotten the defection on the former trip, and he was in no mood to risk it again.

In Phil. 4:6, Paul admonished the Philippians, "Be careful [i.e., anxious] for nothing." "Be careful" is from μεριμνᾶτε, present imperative of μεριμνάω, to be anxious. The meaning is, "Stop being constantly worried about nothing." The Philippians were evidently given to much worry, hence this injunction.

The ten virgins "all slumbered and slept." (Matt. 25:5.) "Slumbered" is from ἐνύσταξαν, aorist indicative, while "slept" is from ἐκάθευδον, imperfect indicative. This distinction is not apparent in the English translation. "They nodded, and then went on sleeping," is the exact force of these verbs. Truly there are many rich and profitable sermons in the Greek tenses awaiting those with sufficient perseverance to dig them out. A preacher who works regularly in the Greek Testament will never find himself wondering what he'll preach on next Sunday!

The tremendous importance of these distinctions in tense, in determining the exact meaning of the sacred text, will appear from an examination of 1 John 3:6, 9. The insuperable difficulty this passage offers to the English reader vanishes immediately on examination of the Greek text. The passage reads:

> "Whosoever abideth in him sinneth not; whosoever sinneth hath not seen him, neither known him. . . . Whosoever is born of God doth not commit sin; for his seed remaineth in him: and he cannot sin, because he is born of God."

Thus rendered, the passage appears to teach that the act of sinning not only excludes from life in Christ and in God, but also indicates that spiritual life has never existed in the one sinning. Yet, the same writer had just penned the words, "If we say we have no sin, we deceive ourselves, and the truth is not in us." (1 John 1:8.) Is there not, in this translation, hopeless and irreconcilable conflict?

The difficulty immediately disappears when one examines the verbs of 1 John 3:6. "Sinneth" is translated from ἁμάρτανει, third person singular, of the present indicative active. The chief characteristic of the present indicative is, as we have seen in Sec. 8, action in progress contemporary with the time of speaking. Because the English language does not distinguish between action in progress in present time, and an act conceived of indefinitely, the force of the tense of the verb *sinneth* as used by John does not appear in the translation. It can be brought to the attention of the English reader only by expanding the translation as follows:

> "Whosoever abideth in him *doth not keep on sinning*" (as he habitually did before his conversion); whosoever *doth keep on sinning* has not seen him, neither known him."

A second difficulty the English version poses likewise disappears on examination of the Greek text. The passage, as translated, seems to say that sinful conduct on the part of an individual is evidence that such a one has *never been saved*, "hath not seen him, neither known him." This is inconsistent with other statements in the same book, and by the same author. He declared that Jesus is our Advocate when we sin, and that if we confess our sins, he will forgive. (1 John 1:9; 2:1, 2.) How is it possible to confess sins never committed? Why do Christians need an Advocate for them when they sin, *if they never sin?*

Here again, the difficulty is only apparent, and is due to a lack of concord in the Greek and English tenses. The verbs "hath (not) seen," and "hath (not) known" are in the perfect tense, ἑώρακεν, ἔγνωκεν. The Greek perfect denotes action absolutely past, which lasts on in its effects. It is thus the function of the perfect to denote the results which follow the action, the action, meanwhile, passing from view. The English perfect, however, keeps the action prominently in view, and in it the past idea predominates; whereas, in Greek the perfect points to the *existing result* following the action.

When one, for example, says, "I have known," the mind instinctively attributes the time of knowing to the past; here, the true significance of the English perfect tense appears. But, in the Greek perfect tense, since the time element is lost sight

49

of, and the force of the tense is to point to an existing state produced by the action, the significance of the statement, "I have known," would be interpreted to mean, "I know now." When the verbs of the sentence are thus given their proper significance, the meaning of the passage, as thus expanded, is, "Whosoever abideth in him does not keep on sinning; whosoever keeps on sinning sees him not, neither knows him." If it is kept in mind that the verbs, *sees* and *knows*, express result, the meaning is clear. Obviously, one who has lapsed into a life of habitual sin no longer sees (enjoys) God, nor knows (recognizes his influence) God in his life.

Once the significance of 1 John 3:6 is recognized, the difficulty in verse 9 disappears. The action of this verse is put in the present infinitive, and not in the aorist tense. We have seen that John did not intend to convey the idea that a child of God cannot commit a single act of sin. The tense used indicates action in progress at the present time:

"Whosoever is born of God doth not keep on committing sin; for his seed remaineth in him, and he cannot keep on committing sin

50

(as a habit) because he is born of God."

Had John intended to teach us that a child of God cannot commit a single act of sin, he would have put the action of this verse in the aorist tense, and would have omitted 1 John 1:9, and 2:1, 2, entirely. He teaches us that a life of habitual sinning is impossible to one in whom the "seed" (the word of God) remains. (Luke 8:11.) David knew this, and said, "Thy word have I hid in my heart that I might not sin against thee." (Ps. 119:11.) John teaches us that one who holds the word of God steadily in view will not, *cannot*, commit sin; it is only when he relinquishes his hold on it, and puts its promptings out of his heart, that he yields to temptation and sin. The "It is written" is as effective in resisting Satan now as it was when the Lord used it so resourcefully on the Mount of Temptation.

EXERCISE 5

1. Before beginning lesson 5, the student should be able to recognize every letter in the Greek alphabet; give the English equivalents; recognize the stem containing the main idea, and to note

how, by the addition of other letters to the stem, case, mood, number, person and tense are indicated. It is not necessary to memorize the forms; we must simply be able to recognize that the different forms exist. The Analytical Lexicon will supply us with all the information we need to know, at this point, regarding meaning and significance, as well as all inflections, of all the words in the Greek New Testament.

2. With Lesson 5, we begin one of the most interesting, as well as one of the most important matters associated with the study of New Testament Greek — the *tenses*. It is vitally important that we note the *difference* in the significance of the tense in English (which notes the *time* element) and that in Greek where it is the *action* of the verb involved, the time element being merely incidental. Memorize the second paragraph (italicized) under Lesson 5, and become thoroughly familiar with the significance of the present tense, the aorist tense, the imperfect tense and the future tense, noting carefully the illustrations given.

3. Note, especially the difference in the significance of Greek and English tenses in the diagram of a

line and a dot, indicating the distinction between the present (an act continuing), and the aorist, (a single act.)

4. See this difference illustrated in our Lord's conversation with the woman at the well in Samaria (John 4:13,14.) Observe the distinction in Mark 2:9; Acts 15:37; Phil. 4:6; Matt. 25:5.

5. Study I John 3:6,9, until thoroughly familiar with the passage, noting the light which a knowledge of Greek sheds on this chapter until every detail is clear.

LESSON 6

PREPOSITIONS

Prepositions are words of location used for the purpose of sharpening the meaning of the cases, and in composition with verbs to heighten and make more vivid the action indicated in the verb. They are used with the "oblique" cases, the Genitive, Dative and Accusative—to make their import more sure. The Genitive is the *Whence* case, the Dative is the *Where* case, and the Accusative is the *Whither* case.

An ordinary arrow will illustrate the functions of these cases and the prepositions used with them in a simple fashion.

Let the feathered portion represent the Genitive—the whence case, suggesting progress *from* some place, thing, etc. The portion of the arrow between the feathered end and the sharp point would represent the Dative, the "resting case," thus suggesting neither motion nor direction, but rest. The spear of the arrow denotes the Accusative, the whither case, indicating direction or motion into a place where it terminates.

Some prepositions govern only the Genitive; others, only the Dative, and still others only the Accusative. Others govern both Genitive and Accusative, and Genitive, Dative and Accusative. A complete table follows:

1. Prepositions governing the Genitive only:
   ἀντί, *instead of, against, for.*
   ἀπό, (from the exterior) *from, away from.*

ἐκ, (from the interior) *from, out of.*
πρό, *before,* (used of time or place.)

2. Prepositions governing the Dative only:
ἐν, *in* (of time, place or element) *among.*
σύν, *with* (cooperation.)

3. Prepositions governing the Accusative only:
εἰς, *into, to, toward, for, among.* (Motion toward, either real or implied.)

4. Prepositions governing the Genitive and Accusative:
διά, Gen. *through, by means of;* Acc. *on account of, or owing to.*
κατά, Gen. *against;* Acc. *along, through, according to.*
μετά, Gen. *together with, among;* Acc. *after.*
περί, Gen. *about, concerning, on behalf of;* Acc. *about, round about.*
ὑπέρ, Gen. *over, above, for, in reference to.* Acc. *beyond, above.*
ὑπό, Gen. *under, by* (instrumental). Acc. *under, close upon.*

5. Prepositions governing the Genitive, Dative, and Accusative:
ἐπι, Gen. *on* (as springing from) *over, in the presence of.*

Dat. *upon*, (as resting on) *in addition to, on account of.*

Acc. *upon, unto, over,* (of time or place.)

παρά, Gen. *from* (used of persons).

Dat. *near* (also of persons).

Acc. *beside, beyond, contrary to.*

πρός, Gen. *towards.*

Dat. *at, close by.*

Acc. *towards, in reference to, with, in consideration of.*

Ἀμφί, *about, around,* is used in the New Testament only in composition. Another thus used is ἀνά, occurring in the sentence, "Understandest thou what thou readest," Ἀρά γε γινώσκεις ἅ ἀνα-γινώσκεις (Acts 8:30), involving a play on words not apparent to the English reader, which we may translate freely as follows: "Do you heed what you read?" σύν often occurs in composition. In it is the idea of association, or cooperation. There are truly many "pictures in prepositions" in the Greek New Testament, and a careful consideration of them will sharpen and vivify our conception of the meaning of many New Testament passages.

The following graphic diagram will exhibit to

the student the primary import of the prepositions. It should be thoroughly mastered.

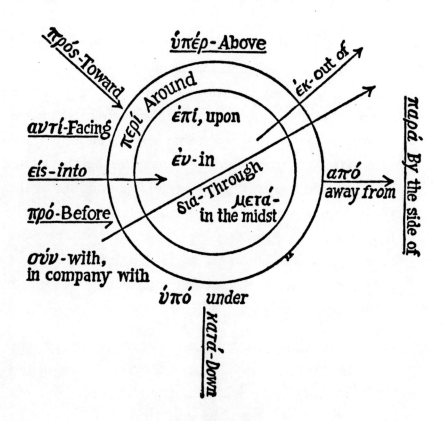

EXERCISE 6

1. Note that prepositions are words of location, and that they make clear the action indicated in the verb. Since they are used with the "oblique" cases to make their significance more obvious, learn that

the Genitive is the *whence* case, the Dative the *where* case, and the Accusative the *whither* case. Master the illustration of the arrow.

2. Read carefully through the prepositions governing the different cases, and become familiar with them. It is, however, not necessary to memorize them at this juncture. Later, we shall need to learn the significance of them, and so be able immediately when they appear, either in composition, or governing verbs, to recognize their meaning. The vivid "pictures in prepositions," abounding in the Greek New Testament constitute an interesting and thrilling study. Note the interesting play on words in Acts 8:30, and the free translation given. The student will soon be able to find many such statements, enriching his concept of the New Testament.

3. Copy the diagram exhibiting the force of the various prepositions, until thoroughly familiar with it. This fully learned, the student will have acquired information he will find useful in every verse of the Greek New Testament.

PART THREE
THE SYSTEM ILLUSTRATED

LESSON 7

If the reader has studied carefully the material in Parts Two and Three, and has mastered the alphabet so as to recognize readily all the Greek letters, he is ready to begin work in the text of the Greek New Testament. Progress, in the beginning, will be slow and laborious, but as he becomes more familiar with the method, and acquires greater facility in handling the Greek Interlinear and the Lexicon, his progress will become more rapid. He is cautioned against superficial effort; it is preferable to master but one verse a day than to pass hurriedly and superficially over a whole chapter. In order to derive real benefit from the effort and to become proficient in the study, every word must be carefully examined, its grammatical relationship noted, traced to its root, and defined. Eventually, the student will become familiar with a large number of words and will be able to recognize them on sight without recourse to the lexicon. The price of success in this study is perseverance.

The two indispensable tools in this effort are (a) The Interlinear Testament, and (b) The

Analytical Greek Lexicon. The study cannot be pursued without these. It will be highly profitable to the student to have available Thayer's Greek English Lexicon, the most authoritative Greek Lexicon in the world, and a Greek Grammar of the New Testament, but for the beginner, and until he has acquired some facility in the study, the Interlinear and The Analytical Greek Lexicon will suffice.*

For our first selection, we shall take the familiar admonition of our Lord in Matt. 7:7: "Ask, and it shall be given you; seek, and ye shall find; knock, and it shall be opened unto you." On turning to this passage in the Greek Interlinear, we discover that it reads as follows:

Αἰτεῖτε, καὶ δοθήσεται ὑμῖν·
ζητεῖτε, καὶ εὑρήσετε·
κρούετε, καὶ ἀνοιγήσεται ὑμῖν·

αἰτεῖτε ** is the first word in the text we have selected for study. We now turn to The Analytical Greek Lexicon, which lists every inflection of every Greek word in the Greek Testament in

* The author will be glad to inform those interested where these may be purchased reasonably.
** Capital letters are omitted at this time to keep the lesson as easily grasped as possible.

its proper alphabetical order, and we find it listed as follows:

αἰτεῖτε 2 pers. pl. pres. imper. act. of αἰτέω. αἰτεῖτε is, then, second person, plural number, present tense, imperative mood, and active voice of the verb αἰτέω. But what is the meaning of αἰτέω? It is defined: *"To ask, request, demand, desire."* The imperative mood indicates to us that it is a command; the present tense that it is action in progress at the present time; and the second person plural that it is addressed to us. The meaning of the word is then, literally, "You keep on asking...."

καὶ is our next word, which the Lexicon lists: "Conj. *and.*"

δοθήσεται comes next. We have this analysis: 3 pers. sing. fut. ind. passive of δίδωμι. The word is thus in the third person, singular number, future tense, indicative mood, and passive voice. Its definition: *"To give, bestow, present."* In keeping with its grammatical analysis, we render it, "it shall be given..."

ὑμῖν is genitive plural of σύ, the pronoun *you, thou.* The first clause of our passage may, therefore, be rendered, *"Keep on asking and it shall be given you."*

ζητεῖτε is the first word of the next clause in our

passage. The Lexicon gives us this information concerning it: 2 pers. pl. pres. imper. act. of ζητέω, *"to seek for, to strive after earnestly."* As in the verb of the preceding clause, the action here is present, and the mood imperative; hence, we render it, *"Keep on earnestly seeking."* Following the conj. *and,* with which we are familiar, and need not look up, having had it already, our next word is εὑρήσετε, 2 pers. plural of the future indicative active of εὑρίσκω, *"to find, discover."* Note the difference of person here and in the preceding clause. There it is third person, *"it"* shall be given; here, it is second person, *"you"* shall find. . . .

κρούετε* is second person plural of the present imperative of κρούω, *"to knock at a door."* (Thayer points out that this word is used to indicate knocking at a door with one's knuckles, being distinguished from κόπτειν, to knock with heavy blows. The word therefore suggests a gentle and reverent, but persistent knocking.)

ἀνοιγήσεται is 3 pers. sing. future passive of ἀνοίγω, *"to open a door."* To open the door to one is, proverbially, to grant that asked for. Thus, those who knock properly before heaven's door are assured that their requests will not be denied.

We now have before us all the information necessary to make our own translation of this passage: *"Keep on asking and it shall be given you; keep on seeking and you shall find; keep on reverently knocking and the door shall be opened unto you."*

By being able to make our own translation of this verse, we have discovered the exact force of the verbs (which we could not have learned from the common versions) ; and we have a richer conception of the terms used than before. Incidental lessons we have learned in the effort are (1) Jesus wants us to persevere in prayer; (2) success will follow such perseverance; and (3) if success does not immediately follow our prayers, we are to persist reverently until it does.

EXERCISE 7

1. Here, at Lesson 7, we begin an analytical study of the Greek Text, in which we shall illustrate the system taught in this book. We shall also see why the Interlinear Greek Testament, and The Analytical Lexicon are necessary to pursue our studies, in

this and the following lessons, we have transferred from those books the necessary information; once the student has become familiar with the system herein taught, he can, by the use of these two volumes, translate the entire New Testament.

2. Copy Matt. 7:7, (following paragraph 3), into notebook, as it appears in the Greek text. Under this verse copy, in large letters, at left margin, the first word. Following it, give person, number, tense, etc., and note word from which it is derived. Designate its definition. Write out free translation. Your arrangement would be somewhat as follows:

Aiteite, second person plural, of the present imperative active of *aiteoo.* (Observe that in spelling *aiteoo,* to indicate that the last letter is Omega — long "o" — we double it.) From the Lexicon learn that the meaning of *aiteoo* (from which our word in the text is derived) means "to ask, request, demand, desire." It is a command, because the mood is imperative; it is in the present tense; therefore, the action is continuous; second person plural is used, so it is addressed to us. Hence, the meaning, "Keeping on asking..."

Our next word is *kai,* which the Lexicon informs us means "and," a conjunction.

Dotheesetai, is 3rd person singular of the future indicative active of *didoomi.* (Note the double "e" to indicate long "e" in *dotheesetai) Didoomi* is defined in the Lexicon "to give, bestow, present." Because the verb is third person singular, and future indicate active, we translate, "It shall be given..." Thus, the clause reads: "Keep asking and it shall be given you."

Humin, is genitive plural of *su.* the pronoun "you," "thou." Observe that in spelling out the Greek word, we begin with the letter "h" because the word is aspirated (See Lesson 3). Note also that through inflection, the pronoun *su,* has become *humin!* Without the Analytical Lexicon, long and laborious study would be required to know all of the inflected forms; by following this study carefully, we shall be able to find them immediately.

Zeeteite is the second person plural of the present imperative active of the verb *zeeteoo.* "to seek for, to strive after earnestly," (so the Lexicon defines it.) The translation, "Keep on earnestly seeking..."

67

Kai, our next word, we have earlier seen, is the conjunction, "and."

Eureesete is second personal plural of the future indicative active of *huriskoo,* "to find, discover." Hence, "you shall find..."

Krouete, second person plural of the present imperative of *krouoo,* to knock at a door."

Anoigeesetai, is 3rd person singular of the future passive of *anoigoo,* "to open a door."

From the information thus gained we can now make our own translation of this passage:

> *"Keep on asking and it shall be given you;*
> *Keep on seeking and you shall find;*
> *Keep on knocking and the door shall be opened*
> *unto you."*

LESSON 8

For our second practice selection, we shall translate the Greek text of Rom. 8:26, which the King James Translators rendered as follows:

"Likewise the Spirit also helpeth our infirmities: for we know not what to pray for as we ought; but the Spirit maketh intercession for us with groanings which cannot be uttered."

The Greek text of this passage reads,

Ὡσαύτως δὲ καὶ τὸ πνεῦμα ούναντιλαμβάνεται ταῖς ἀσθενείαις ἡμῶν· τὸ γὰρ τί προσευξώμεθα καθὸ δεῖ οὐκ οἴδαμεν αλλ᾿ αὐτό τὸ πνεῦμα ὑπερεντυγχάνει ὑπὲρ ἡμῶν στεναγμοῖς ἀλαλήτοις·

By referring to our Analytical Lexicon, we learn that the words of the first clause are analyzed and defined as follows:

Ὡσαύτως, adverb, *"Just so, in the same way or manner, likewise."*

δε, "A particle marking the superaddition of a clause."

Its meaning: *"but, on the other hand, also."*

τό πνεῦμα, the Spirit, i.e., the Holy Spirit.

αὐτό, *himself.**

* "The Spirit" is neuter gender here, grammatically, but in John 16:13, 26 the pronoun is masculine. It is a serious mistake to refer to the Holy Spirit as "it," or "itself." The Spirit is a masculine personality, and should always be referred to as such.

συναντιλαμβάνεται, 3 pers. sing. pres. ind. act. of συναντιλαμβάνομαι. This word is a compound verb, from λαμβάνω, *to take hold of,* σύν, *together, with,* and ἀντί, *on the opposite side, over against.* It is of interest to observe that this verb occurs only one other time in the Greek Testament—in the narrative of Luke 10:40, when Martha, vexed and cumbered with much serving, and annoyed because of Mary's uncooperativeness, asked Jesus to bid Mary to *help,* συναντιλάβηται, literally, to "Stand over on the opposite side from me, and take hold of the work, so that the two of us working together can get the job done!"

Was Martha attempting to move a heavy table at the very moment she addressed these words to the Savior? Did she also point to the table when she requested Jesus to bid Mary to take hold on the other side and help her? We may well believe that such was so, for this is the picture drawn for us in the Greek verb. The Spirit helps us—he stands over against us, as it were, and lifts with us until by our united efforts our burdens are lifted.

ταῖς, the definite article, dat. case, masculine gender.

ἀσθενία, dative plural of ἀσθενής, *suffering, affliction, distress, calamity.*

ἡμῶν, genitive plural, signifying here, *our.*

Our translation, slightly expanded, to indicate the full significance of the terms, runs: *"Likewise also the Spirit takes hold along with us, and helps us bear our earthly afflictions. . . ."*

We are now ready for the second clause of this passage:

τὸ, the article, indicating that the whole clause is the object of *"we know."*

γὰρ, conjunction, *for.*

τί, *that.*

προσευξώμεθα, 1 pers. pl. fut. indicative of προσεύχομαι, *to pray, to offer prayer.*

καθὸ, *how, in what manner.*

δεῖ, *"it is necessary, it behoveth, it is proper."*

οὐκ, adverb of negation, *not, no.*

οἴδαμεν, 1 pers. pl. of οἶδα, *to know.*

Our translation, of this clause, again expanded,

71

to suggest the force of the terms: *"For what to pray—what is proper for our needs, we know not . . ."*

Concluding our analysis of the passage, we shall analyze the final clause:

αλλ᾽, conjunction, *but, however, still more.* The word also serves to introduce a thought with keenness and emphasis.

αὐτό, Nom. sing. neuter of αὐτός, *self.*

τὸ πνεῦμα, the Spirit.

ὑπερεντυγχάνει, 3 pers. sing. pres. ind. of ὑπερεντυγχάνω, "to intercede for." This, too, is a compound word, composed of τυγχάνω, *to happen;* ἐν, *in;* and ὑπέρ, *in behalf of;* hence, literally, to happen in just in the nick of time, for our assistance. How comforting it is, when exhausted and weary from heavy burdens, to have a friend or brother come along, and lend a willing hand until the task is done. Such is the picture presented us in this verb of the Holy Spirit's aid.

ὑπέρ, prep. *"in behalf of."*

ἡμῶν, pronoun, gen. plural of ἐμός, possessive *my, mine.*

στεναγμοῖς, dat. plural of στεναγμός, *inward sighing, groaning.*

αλαλήτοις, dat. pl. masculine of ἀλάλητος, *unutterable, unexpressed.* Sighs not expressed in words.

Our task is finished, and we may gather up the full translation, thus:

> "Likewise also the Spirit takes hold along with us, and helps us bear our earthly afflictions; what to pray for—what is proper for our needs—we know not, but the Spirit himself intercedes for us with unutterable sighs."

It is, of course, possible for one to search through the critical commentaries and learn the manner in which the spirit "aids" us, but such a task is a slow, tedious and tiresome one. Here, in a mere matter of moments, we have learned the same truth, by a brief and easy examination of the Greek text. Such an examination will always pay rich dividends in increased knowledge and vividness of detail. It should never be neglected.

EXERCISE 8

1. In chapter 8, we have our second practice selection — Rom. 8:26. As in the preceding lesson,

copy the Greek text into your notebook, using care to make the Greek letters properly, spelling them correctly, and affixing all necessary marks.

2. Here, again, we have supplied from the Analytical Lexicon an analysis of every Greek word in the passage. The student should, as in Lesson 7, transfer these to his notebook, giving the full grammatical analysis. Copy, also, the exegetical comments as these will greatly increase our knowledge of the passage.

3. When each word has been analyzed, write out your own free translation of the passage.

4. The effort will, of course, be slow and laborious in the beginning; but, with practice, the student will become more proficient, and eventually be able, with the aid of the Interlinear and the Analytical Lexicon, to make his way with ease anywhere in the Greek Testament.

LESSON 9

Often one will not have the time to make a word for word translation of the passage being studied, but is interested in ascertaining the meaning of some word or phrase therein. In such instances, the Greek Testament may always be examined with great profit. It is often impossible to suggest the full meaning of the sacred writer in the few words possible in translation. Even the Translators of our versions in popular use were not always able to do so, and frequently were forced to resort to the use of many words in order to indicate the meaning of one word in the Greek text. *Five* words in English translate the one Greek word συνεργοῦντες in 2 Cor. 6:1.

In all knotty matters of exegesis, the Greek text may be consulted with great pleasure and profit, and the careful student may, in this manner, greatly illumine the sacred writings for present-day readers. Often, it is possible to suggest lessons not apparent in any other way.

As an example, we read that "the law was our *schoolmaster* to bring us to Christ." (Gal. 3:24.) Were one, in attempting to ascertain the exact meaning of the word "schoolmaster," to consult the Dictionary, he would find that he is "a man who teaches a school; one of the masters of a school." With this definition, one might then conclude that Paul is teaching us that it was the function of the law to serve as a *teacher* of the Israelite people, through whose instruction they were led to Christ. Such is, in no sense, the idea

75

intended by Paul. The word "schoolmaster" is translated from the Greek παιδαγωγός, a servant in control of children, empowered with the responsibility of escorting them to the schoolhouse door where, when they were placed in the care of the teacher, his responsibility ended. There is some resemblance between this individual and the school bus driver of today; and without doing too much injustice to Paul's idea, we may paraphrase thus: "The law was a school bus driver to escort the Jews to Christ." After that Christ came, the functions of the παιδαγωγός ended. (Gal. 3:25.) When it became possible for the Jews to enroll in the School of Christ, the services of the *school bus driver* (the law of Moses) were no longer needed.

Valuable lessons, not apparent to the English reader, will be seen in Paul's use of the present and aorist tenses in Romans 6. In chapter 5, he had argued at length that where "sin abounded, grace did much more abound." (Rom. 5:20.) Enemies of Paul and the gospel—the Judaizing teachers—wrested the inference from this that Paul was licensing people to sin by such reasoning. If grace was always sufficient to surpass sin, why not sin the more in order that grace might more abound? Did not such teaching lead to, and en-

courage a life of sin? So his enemies affirmed. Answered Paul, "Shall we continue . . . ἐπιμένωμεν,
present tense of the word μένω, to remain—shall
we settle down as if at home in a state of sin?" *God
forbid.* The thought itself was a horrible one to
the apostle. Moreover, the idea was an absurd one,
because Paul and the Christians of whom he wrote
had died—separated themselves from a life of sin.
It was therefore utter folly to imagine that one
could continue in a life of sin from which he had
been separated by death. (Rom. 6:2-4.) But, the
false teacher might object that Paul's argument
did not forbid occasional indulgence in sin, even
if it were conceded that a life of sin—of habitual
sin—had been terminated. This alternative Paul
met with the aorist subjunctive: "What then?
Shall we sin, ἁμαρτήσωμεν, Shall we commit *a
single act* of sin because we are not under law,
but under grace?" Here, the word translated *sin*
is an ingressive aorist. The apostle shows that this
alternative suggested by the false teacher does not
follow because he who yields to sin becomes in
the first indulgence a slave to sin. Christians have
been delivered from such bondage. (Rom. 6:15-
19.) Paul is not arguing that a child of God *cannot* commit a single act of sin; he is contending
that he will not submit to occasional acts of sin

77

on the assumption that the grace of God makes provision for such deliberate acts. The idea is repulsive.

A difficulty which appears in the English text of Gal. 6:2, 5, of serious proportions, vanishes following a mere glance at the Greek text. "Bear ye one another's burdens," said the apostle in verse 2. Yet, in verse 5, he says, "For every man shall bear his own burden." How can we bear each other's burdens, if each is to bear his own burden? The word "burden" in verse 2 is βάρη, an overload. We are to assist our brethren in bearing the crushing burdens of life which would, without such assistance, crush the bearer; yet "every man shall bear his own burden," φορτίον, his own pack. φορτίον was used in the first century of the pack or load which the soldier carried on the march. In Matt. 11:30, Jesus uses it to describe the daily burdens which Christians must carry. Though we may aid our brethren in bearing the overtaxing weights which sometimes descend upon them, each must assume and bear his own pack (responsibility) in life. In verse 2, the word βάρη thus indicates our duty to lend a hand to help our brethren bear the heavy loads of life while in verse 5, φορτίον points to the burden common to all Christians, and which each must bear and not attempt to shift to the shoulders of another. The apostle is telling us that we should aid our brethren in the unusual difficulties which beset them, and to carry our own load in life with patience and fortitude. The English translation does not reveal that two different Greek words are translated by the one English word *burden*.

When the Syro-Phoenician woman approached the Savior in behalf of her sick daughter, it is reported that he answered, "It is not meet to take the children's bread and cast it unto the dogs." (Mark 7:27.) This language shocks us. Then, even more so than now, the dog was regarded as a semi-savage animal, a scavenger of the streets, living by its wits, vicious, bold, repulsive in nature. In being likened to dogs, how could this woman have regarded our Lord's words as anything other than Pharisaic and bigoted? Why did she not turn from him in disgust in having herself and sick child so characterized? The word Jesus used is κυνάρια, diminutive, meaning "little dogs," or *puppies!* Puppies were children's pets, they had the run of the house, and from under the table where the children ate they feasted on the crumbs which fell from their hands. The Syro-Phoenician woman, far from being insulted at our Lord's remark, accepted his characterization, and

79

skillfully turned it into an argument in her favor. Said she, "Yes, Lord: yet the puppies under the table eat of the children's crumbs." Touched by this attitude of sweet reasonableness, Jesus answered, "O woman, great is thy faith: be it unto thee even as thou wilt." (Matt. 15:28.)

EXERCISE 9

1. We will not always have the time or the inclination to make a word-for-word translation of every passage in which we are interested; but, we shall often wish to study certain words or phrases in the Greek Text; and, Lesson 9 provides us with numerous examples of the value of such study. Let the student remember that with practice he can, when this work is finished, study any verse in the Greek Testament in the manner demonstrated in this lesson.

2. Copy, into your notebook, each Greek word in this chapter; and, under it write out in your own words the comments, giving particular attention to light shed on these verses by looking into the Greek text. If the student is perplexed by references to terms not thusfar met with in these studies, he will find a complete and easy analysis in the introduction to the Analytical Lexicon.

This course does not affect to be a Greek Grammar; it is designed for those who know no Greek, whatsoever; but, who wish to study the words of Inspiration as they were originally written.

LESSON 10

An examination of the Greek text often guards one against falling into common errors of interpretation. It is, for example, generally believed that the apostle Peter was guilty of *profanity* when he denied the Lord, because the English text says that "He began to curse and to swear." (Mark 14: 71.) This interpretation does the apostle gross injustice, and does not correctly represent his conduct on that fateful occasion. The conclusion that Peter indulged in profanity is reached because some interpret words in their current usage, which is often quite different from that which obtained when the King James Translation was made in 1611; and because the interpreter does not look into the Greek text to ascertain what the Holy Spirit says actually occurred.

It is of course true that the words "curse" and "swear" indicate profanity today; but it must also

81

be remembered that Mark did not write in English, but in Greek; and that these words are translations of the original. The word "curse" is the rendering of the Greek ἀναθεματίζω, "to declare anathema or accursed, to devote to destruction." (Thayer.) In Mark 14:71, this lexicographer says that the word means "to asseverate with direful imprecations." The apostle, in denying any association with Jesus, enforced his denial by calling down upon his head divine curses if what he was saying was not true. The word occurs in Acts 23: 12, where it is said that certain Jews bound themselves "under a *curse*" declaring that they would neither eat nor drink until they had killed Paul.

"Swear," in Mark 14:71, is from ὀμνύω, "to swear; to affirm, promise, threaten, with an oath." (Thayer.) When Jehovah took an oath that what he said is true, this is the word used. (Heb. 6:13.) Thus, when Peter denied his Lord, he did not give utterance to vile and obscene language, as many think. His sin in denying the Lord of glory was a grievous one, and he added to its gravity by taking an oath that what he was saying was true, but he did not resort to profanity.

That gigantic ecclesiastical organization, the Roman Catholic Church, attempts to sustain its claim of apostolicity by disregarding the *gender* of two nouns in Matt. 16:18. Here, Jesus said to Peter, "Thou art Peter, and upon this rock I will build my church; and the gates of Hell shall not prevail against it." *Peter* is a proper noun, translated from the Greek πέτρος. *Rock* is a common noun, the rendering of πέτρα. In view of the fact that the two nouns are of the same derivation, it is the contention of the papacy that Jesus, in this passage, declared his intention of building the church on the apostle Peter, and that this apostle was indeed the rock on which the church was built. They allege that the force of our Lord's words in this passage is this: "Peter, you are a rock, and upon you I propose to build my church."

This argument, carrying on its face a degree of plausibility, breaks down under investigation. πέτρος, translated *Peter,* is masculine gender; whereas πέτρα, rendered *rock,* is feminine gender. To indicate the distinction of gender here, one might render, "Peter you are a *he-rock;* but upon this *she-rock* I will build my church!" Thus understood, and correctly so, one could never conclude that Peter is the foundation of the church. The *rock* on which the church is founded is the truth Peter confessed when he said, "Thou art the Christ, the Son of the living God." (Matt. 16:16.) Moreover, there is a distinction of meaning in the

83

two terms. πέτρα is a massive living rock, while πέτρος is a detached fragment. (Thayer.) Peter was a mere *pebble* compared with the massive foundation of truth—the deity of Jesus—on which the church is built.

Paul, in his Letter to the church in Philippi, assured the brethren that the things which had happened to him had "fallen out rather to the *furtherance* of the gospel." (Phil. 1:12.) The word "furtherance," from προκοπὴν, accusative singular of προκοπή, metaphorically, "advancement, progress, furtherance," was used in the first century of the work of men who went in advance of an army and cut out the largest trees that the army might move through without hindrance. Paul thus regarded his trials as divine *wood-cutters*, preparing the way for the advance of the gospel! This genuinely Christian philosophy all of us might well adopt!

John said that he who "transgresseth and abideth not in the doctrine of Christ, hath not God." (2 John 9.) "Transgresseth" in this passage is from προάγων, nominative case, singular number, masculine gender, present participle of προάγω "to go ahead." From this root are derived our English words, *progress, progressive, progression.* One is indeed progressive when he goes be-

84

yond that which is written. In some matters it is far better not to be progressive—particularly in not going beyond what the Lord has said.

In 2 Cor. 3:18, Paul wrote, "But we all, with open face beholding as in a glass the glory of the Lord, are *changed* into the same image from glory to glory even as by the Spirit of the Lord." The verb "changed" in this passage, is from μεταμορφούμεθα, first person plural of the present indicative passive of μεταμορφόω, which Bagster says is "to undergo a spiritual transformation," and Thayer comments that "we are transformed into the same image (of consummate excellence that shines in Christ) reproduce the same image." From *metamorpho*, we derive our English word "metamorphosis," a term descriptive of the biological change which occurs when a caterpillar shuffles out of its ugly shell, and emerges as a butterfly. This term, Paul uses to describe the transformation that takes place in the child of God as he lays aside his carnal, fleshly nature, and emerges in the likeness of Christ. He is metamorphosed into the Divine Image, and is henceforth to live and be like the Lord. The term also occurs in Rom. 12:2, where it is rendered "transformed," and in Matt. 17:2, where it is said that Jesus was "transfigured." It is a vivid figure of transformation.

The careful student of the word who has established the habit of looking regularly into the Greek Testament in knotty matters of exegesis will avoid the common errors of interpretation characteristic of the immature and the inexperienced. Those among his hearers who are well informed in the Word will at once perceive that he is not a novice in biblical exegesis. His more vivid insight into the sacred writings will enable him to inform, edify and inspire his listeners with lessons from the Word of God beyond the reach of those who lack the equipment for such endeavor. Such an expositor will never stumble into the glaring errors so often made by those unacquainted with the Greek text.

For example, he would not teach that "the church *of the first-born*" (Heb. 12:23) is synonymous with "the church *of the Lord*" in Acts 20:28. He knows that "first-born" is from πρωτοτόκων, genitive *plural* of πρωτότοκος, first-born, literally, *first-born ones*. For the same reason he will not teach that the word "dead" in the passage, "Else what shall they do which are baptized for the dead, if the dead rise not at all? why are they then baptized for the dead?" (1 Cor. 15:29), refers to

Christ, however attractive such an explanation might be, and however much it might serve to remove a difficulty of the most formidable nature. The word *dead* in the passage is from νεκρῶν, genitive *plural* of νεκρός, *dead,* literally, *dead ones.*

He is aware of the fact that in the passage, "He came unto his *own,* and his *own* received him not" (John 1:11), the first *own* does not refer to the same thing as the second. He came into his own country or land ("ἴδια, neuter plural), and his own people (οἱ ἴδιοι, masculine plural) received him not.

He would never charge Paul with actually wishing that he might be declared anathema by Christ if in so doing his brethren after the flesh might be saved. (Rom. 9:3.) When Paul said, "For I could wish that myself were accursed from Christ for my brethren, my kinsmen according to the flesh," he did not express a desire for that which he had no right to feel—a willingness to be lost himself if in so doing his brethren after the flesh— the Israelites—might be saved. The word is ηὐχόμην, imperfect indicative of εὔχομαι, a wish. The imperfect tense indicates that the apostle was about to wish for that to which he had no right; and that he drew back when the realization of this fact dawned upon him. "I was just about to wish

87

..." is the significance of the verb he uses. While Paul had a great yearning for the salvation of his people, he did not commit the grave moral wrong of desiring spiritual suicide to win the Jews to Christ. It is a grave error for biblical expositors to represent him as so doing.

The apostle Peter in his statement, "Likewise, ye wives, be in subjection to your own husbands: that, if any obey not the word, they also may *without the word* be won by the conversation of the wives" (1 Peter 3:1), is not minimizing the importance of the written Word of God. He is not suggesting that stubborn, rebellious, disobedient husbands may be brought to the truth *without the word* of truth. Such an idea is self-contradictory. In no other way can individuals be brought to the truth except by the truth. What, then, is the meaning of this passage? In the phrase, "if any obey not the word," *the word* is τῷ λόγῳ. (Note the use of the article τῷ, *the* before λόγῳ, *word*.) But, in the phrase, "without the word," the article, *the*, does not appear. The first occurrence of λόγος is said to be *articular* (with the article), the second is *anarthrous* (without the article). The Authorized Version does not recognize this fact and places the definite article in the English translation where it does not occur in the Greek. Here, where the definite article does not occur, the indefinite article should be used. The passage would then read, "Likewise ye wives, be in subjection to your own husbands: that, if any obey not the word, they also may *without a word* be won by the conversation (literally, manner of life) of the wives."

Those wives whose husbands have repeatedly heard the word of God, and yet have refused to obey it, are not to importune and persuade constantly lest such should descend to the level of nagging, and defeat the very purpose for which it is done. Instead, they are to live such godly lives before them that *without an additional word* from the wife, the hitherto rebellious husband will be influenced to obey that which he knows is right. Peter does not nullify the Word. These husbands knew the truth, but would not obey it. He hence urges that the wives refrain from further importunity and by godly living influence the will of those whose judgment was already convinced.

The "eye of a needle" (Matt. 19:24) through which it is impossible for a camel to pass was not, many expositors to the contrary notwithstanding, a gate by that name in the wall of the city of Jerusalem. Neither has an error crept into the text by which κάμηλος, a camel, has been substituted for κάμιλος, a seaman's cable, as some think. Luke has, for the word needle, Βελόγης, a surgeon's needle. (Luke 18:25.) The careful and sincere student will not attempt to assist the Lord out of difficulties into which the uninformed would plunge him through unskilled and erroneous interpretation.

The two criminals who were crucified with Jesus were not *thieves,* men who, under cover of darkness and by stealth, filch that which belongs to others, but λησταί, robbers, men who took the property of others by force. Thayer adds the note on the foregoing word that it is "not to be confounded with κλέπτης, thief, one who takes property by stealth (although the distinction is obscured in the Authorized Version.) " (Matt. 27: 38.)

The Greek Testament (but not our common versions) distinguishes between the sacred edifice of the temple, and its enclosures. ναός is the term used to refer to the building, ἱερόν to the premises thereof. The Lord is never said to have entered into the ναός, but always the ἱερόν. Into the sanctuary, consisting of a holy place, and a most holy place separated by a veil, only the priests could enter, the common priests being allowed to enter the first compartment—the holy place—and the high priests alone being privileged to enter the most holy place, once a year on the occasion of the great day of Atonement. Inasmuch as Jesus was of the tribe of Judah (Heb. 7:14), and the Law of Moses provided that priests must be of the tribe of Levi (Heb. 7:11), he could not qualify as a priest under the law (Heb. 8:4), and was thus never in the temple proper. When it is said that Jesus, or the apostles, "went up" or "entered" the temple, the word is always ἱερόν, and never ναός. This important distinction, obscured in the translations, but obvious to the Greek student, enables us to understand how money-changers were said to be in the temple. They were not in the consecrated and hallowed building, but in one of the enclosures surrounding the sacred edifice. (Matt. 21:12; John 5:14; Acts 3:2.) Zacharias was "slain between the temple and the altar," and if we are made to wonder how this could be since the altar was in the temple enclosure, the matter is cleared up by the fact that the word for temple in this passage (Matt. 23:35) is ναός, the temple proper, being distinguished from its courts and premises. Evidently, the brazen altar was not in the ναός, but in the ἱερόν, i.e., in one of the courts of the ναός.

The "mystery" of the gospel of Christ (Greek, μυστήριον) is not "something that has not been, or cannot be explained; hence, something beyond

91

human comprehension" (Webster), but in the New Testament is "God's plan of providing salvation for men through Christ, which was once hidden but is now revealed." (Rom. 16:25; 1 Cor. 2:7; Eph. 3:9; Col. 1:26.) (Thayer.)

The word διάκονος, whence comes our word *deacon*, occurs many times in the New Testament, and its usual significance is a servant or minister. (Mark 10:43; Matt. 23:11.) In the so-called official sense it occurs in Phil. 1:1; 1 Tim. 3:8, 12; Acts 6:3 (in the Greek.) Some authorities trace its origin from διά and κόνις, literally, "to kick up dust by hastening." (Let the deacons take notice!) Thayer questions this derivation. The word occurs in feminine form in Rom. 16:1, where it is said that Phoebe was a servant (literally, a deaconness) of the church in Cenchreae.

Despite a widely prevalent view to that end, the word *nature* in the passage, "And were by nature the children of wrath, even as others" (Eph. 2:3), does not denote *original,* or *inbred* sin. It is translated from the Greek φύσις, which Thayer says is "a mode of feeling and acting which by long habit has become nature." Our provincial word, "second nature," is an approximation of its meaning. The word occurs in Paul's reference to nature teaching that if a man have long hair it is a shame unto him.

(1 Cor. 11:14.) If *nature* here is that which one receives from his parents, it should be unnecessary for a man whose father was bald ever to go to the barber shop to have his hair trimmed!

EXERCISE 10

This lesson contains many interesting and thrilling side-lights drawn from the study of the Greek Text. Copy each passage; the words involved, and the comments given. This is good practice; and it will provide the student with easy familiarity with the proper procedure for such studies, when he has obtained the Interlinear and the Analytical Lexicon, and has begun his own independent studies in the sacred text.

LESSON 11

A minute and detailed study of the Greek text, though laborious and tiring, never fails to yield large results to those with the perseverance and determination sufficient to the effort. For example, it is highly instructive to observe that in the expression "good works," the adjective *good* only partially suggests the meaning couched in the

Greek καλός. The word "good" is limited to the description of moral quality, whereas, καλός means not only that which is good, but also that which is *beautiful,* harmonious, lovely, symmetrical. Works, in order to be good in God's sight, must also be beautiful; and it matters not how much one's life may conform to the laws of moral rectitude, it is imperfect unless it also measures to the law of beauty, i.e., to beautiful conduct. We are just as obligated to make our lives attractive and beautiful to others as we are to make them pure. He who exhibits a stern, unbending disposition, though his life be an exemplary one, is lacking in the qualities which are described in the Bible as *good.* (Matt. 5:16; 26:10; Mark 14:6; 1 Tim. 3:1.)

The vividness of the original is so much sharper than the translation when Jesus bade the sinful woman who anointed his feet at Simon's feast to "go *into* peace." πορεύου εἰς εἰρήνην. (Luke 7:50.) The A.V. has the greatly weakened rendering, "go *in* peace." To go *in* peace is to enjoy merely momentary respite from trouble, toil, anxiety; to go *into* peace is to pass, as it were, into a realm where peace may be one's constant, treasured possession and companion.

In the phrase, "looking unto Jesus," in Hebrews 12:2, the verb is not the usual Greek word for looking, but a compound of the preposition ἀπό, and ἀφορῶντες. This word means "to turn the eyes away from other things and fix them on something." (Thayer.) The English reader gets only half of the meaning intended by the sacred writer. Not only did he tell us to look *to* Jesus, he also bids us look *away* from everything else! In looking to Jesus, the Hebrews were to look away from the world, its allurements, the shame of the cross, the cloud of witnesses, indeed everything that would distract their attention or hinder their progress in the Christian race.

In three prepositions, Paul presents a picture of the atonement which Jesus has provided. (Gal. 3:10-13.) He declares that all who seek to be saved by the law are *under* (ὑπό) a curse: "For as many as are of the works of the law are under the curse." (Verse 10.) He then informs us that Christ became a curse *for* (ὑπέρ) us: "Christ hath redeemed us from the curse of the law, being made a curse for us." (Verse 13.) As a result, we have been brought *out* from under (ἐκ) the curse of the law: "Christ hath redeemed us from the curse of the law." We were delivered out (ἐκ) from under (ὑπό) the law because Christ allowed the curse of the law to fall upon him in our stead. (ὑπέρ.) The word *redeem* (ἐξαγοράζω) was often used in the first century of those who went into the slave markets and purchased the liberty of those enslaved. Our Lord went into the slave market of sin, and with his own precious blood as the purchase price, obtained our freedom from the bondage of sin. As it was common in those days for a man to purchase a slave for the purpose of freeing him, so did Jesus buy us with his blood that we might be free. Hence Paul admonishes us "to stand fast in the liberty (freedom) wherewith Christ hath made us free." (Gal. 5:1.) It was *Christ* who freed us, and to him are we eternally indebted for the freedom we enjoy.

In the King James Version, three Greek words are translated by the one English word, *hell*. In "hell," the rich man lifted up his eyes (Luke 16:23) ; God spared not the angels that sinned, but "cast them down to hell" (2 Peter 2:4) ; and one who says to his brother, "thou fool," is in danger of "hell fire." (Matt. 5:22.) In each of these passages the word *hell* is the rendering of a different Greek word. The rich man lifted up his eyes in ἁδης, the realm of departed spirits; the angels who sinned were cast down to τάρταρος, the abode of wicked spirits between death and the resurrection; and the "hell fire," of Matt. 5:22, is γέεννα, the lake of fire and brimstone, which is the second death, awaiting the finally impenitent. These distinctions, immediately apparent to those who examine the Greek Testament, are totally obscured in the English translation most commonly in use, with the result that one could never know the exact significance of these passages by following the common version alone.

Inspiration extends to the words of scripture, and we must not be satisfied until we have plumbed their depths, and scaled their heights to the best of our ability. The Holy Spirit guided the apostles and sacred writers in their selection of terms necessary to convey the meaning of the Spirit, and it is our solemn duty and glorious privilege to draw out from them their rich and choicest lessons. Nothing less than the best we have to offer to such studies will suffice; and with nothing less should we be satisfied. Such efforts, brought to the study and exposition of the Scriptures, though laborious and slow, will result in increased power and penetration; in more appreciation of the word of God and the message of life and salvation; and they will enable one to become more accurate, effective and skilled in expounding the precious

Words of Life to perishing humanity. To its accomplishment no effort is too great, no task too weighty. It is a goal toward which every teacher of the divine oracles should strive.

EXERCISE 11

Lesson 11 though shorter, contains a more extended treatment of the words involved; and it should be studied until every word, in Greek, and in English, is familiar. Copy the comments into the notebook and refer to them often in the study of these words and phrases as they appear in other passages.

PART FOUR

THE SYSTEM APPLIED

LESSON 12

When the materials of interpretation have been assembled, they must be arranged and evaluated correctly. Though one has at his finger tips all the information necessary to determine the meaning of the text in which he is interested, he may fail of its correct interpretation by unskilled methods and defective arrangement. The observance of a few simple, but absolutely essential, rules of interpretation will aid one immeasurably in arriving at the correct meaning of the text being studied.

1. The interpretation must be *lexical*. One must know the etymology of the words, their development historically, and their use in the period and passage under consideration. This information may be obtained from the lexicons. There is much unskilled use of Greek lexicons these days. Many would-be interpreters consult the lexicon, and from the many definitions given, select the one most in harmony with *their* idea of the meaning of the word, and disregard utterly the lexicographer's own selection of the word in the passage.

In the use of the lexicons, one must note the meaning of the word under study at different

101

periods of the Greek language, and in the different authors of the same period. Further, he must note whether the lexicon he uses gives the classical meaning or the N.T. meaning of the word. There may be, and often is, a vast difference in the two. For example the word δαιμόνιον, *a demon*, meant in early Greek, a departed spirit; Socrates thought it was a guardian spirit; in the New Testament, it is a wicked spiritual being producing mental and physical disorders in human beings. Josephus, the Jewish historian, used it in the sense of a deity, or divinity. It is used once in the New Testament in this sense, "He seemeth to be a setter forth of strange gods" (ξένων δαιμονίον) , strange demons. (Acts 17:18.)

A good all-purpose lexicon of New Testament Greek is Thayer's Greek English Lexicon of the New Testament.* It has been approximately 80 years since it was revised, however; and it does not reflect the results of study in the contemporary literature of the apostolic age which has been very extensive during this period. It was formerly believed that the New Testament Greek was a "biblical language," possessing peculiarities all its own; and Thayer lists about fourteen columns of sixty words each which he alleges are "biblical words,"

102

* Most Greek students today prefer a Greek English Lexicon by Arndt and Gingrich.

i.e., found nowhere else in Greek literature except in the Bible. Since the last revision of Thayer, nearly all of these words have been found in the *papyri,* that great mass of literature and life of the common people of the first centuries which came to light about the last decade of the last century. It is now believed that the New Testament Greek is the same as that used in the business, social and economic world of the first years of the Christian Era, and an examination of the use of such terms as are common to that usage and to the Bible sheds much light on their meaning. Huge amounts of *papyri* were discovered in Egypt about 1890, and these were all written in a type of Greek very similar to that of the New Testament. One who would work with the very latest of such information available would have Moulton and Milligan's Vocabulary of the New Testament Illustrated from the Papyri, a monumental work, but too scholarly and expensive for the beginner. The best *classical* lexicon of Greek is Liddell and Scott. (Unabridged.)

2. Interpretation, to be correct, must be *grammatical.* The working student will have available, if possible, two or three good grammars of N.T. Greek to consult in problems of syntax. To be a

skilled and accurate translator, one must not only know the structure of the Greek language, he must also be familiar with its forms and modes of expression, and this he can learn only from the grammars of the language.

3. The *context* must be considered in interpretation. It is an old adage that a *text,* taken from its *context,* becomes a mere *pretext!* This is particularly true in the realm of biblical exegesis. Occasionally, meanings are attributed to passages which are directly opposite that intended by the writer. A good example is Col. 2:21, "Touch not, taste not, handle not." This is often used as a text for a temperance sermon. In truth, Paul is saying (as the context reveals) , "Don't let people tell you that you cannot touch, taste, handle. . . ." It is a condemnation of ascetic practices, and does not remotely touch the question of the use of intoxicating drink.

4. Finally one must interpret *historically.* He must seek, as far as possible, to reproduce in his mind the circumstances which prompted the writing of the statement he is studying. The manners, customs, history, government, psychology, and a hundred other matters combine to create the

historical background. The commentaries are designed to assist the student in reconstructing for himself the circumstances under which the writer penned his words.

In using the commentaries, the student must be careful not to fall into a very common, and fatal error, of examining several, and then from the number accepting the interpretation which pleases him most. Such a method is bad procedure for several reasons. In the first place, by it one is tempted to accept the interpretation which fits in with his preconceived opinions, without regard to the facts which should be carefully weighed before a conclusion is reached; and secondly, it establishes the habit of trying to remember all of the interpretations given, and using these, without arriving at a definite conclusion as to the meaning of the text. If one is not careful, he learns simply to parrot the explanations given by the scholars, and never forms an independent opinion of his own. Where the commentaries differ—as they frequently do—he finds himself without guidance, and therefore confused as to the meaning and significance of the passage in which he is interested.

The correct exegetical procedure is (1) What has the author said? and (2) What does he mean?

What he has said may be ascertained from the text, *properly translated;* what he means will be determined by the rules of exegesis outlined hereinbefore. The commentaries should then be consulted for the purpose of checking one's own interpretation, and for any additional light they may throw upon the text not in the possession of the student. In the use of the commentaries, (and there are many good ones available today), the student must ever keep in mind the theological prepossessions of the writer, and remember that his interpretations are colored and influenced by his religious position.

EXERCISE 12

Here, in the final lesson in the series, is taught how to assemble and to evaluate the materials of our translation properly. The subject matter in this chapter is vital to any proper interpretation of the scriptures. Master it fully.

If you have followed these studies with reasonable thoroughness and attention; and, if you will utilize your knowledge in the use of the Greek Testament, and the Lexicon, you have before you the prospect of one of life's most thrilling experiences. May God's richest blessings attend you in the study of His Word!

SCRIPTURE INDEX